Find your way with words

Making Better Sentences

Rebecca Vickers

Raintree is an imprint of Capstone Global Library
Limited, a company incorporated in England and
Wales having its registered office at 7 Pilgrim
Street, London, EC4V 6LB – Registered company
number: 6695582

www.raintreepublishers.co.uk
myorders@raintreepublishers.co.uk

Edited by Andrew Farrow, Laura Hensley,
Vaarunika Dharmapala, Helen Cox Cannons
Designed by Philippa Jenkins
Original illustrations © Capstone Global Library
Ltd
Illustrated by Capstone Global Library Ltd
Picture research by Tracy Cummins
Production by Sophia Argyris
Printed in China by Leo Paper Products Ltd

ISBN 978 1 406 26161 5 (hardback)
17 16 15 14 13
10 9 8 7 6 5 4 3 2 1

ISBN 978 1 406 26166 0 (paperback)
18 17 16 15 14
10 9 8 7 6 5 4 3 2

British Library Cataloguing in Publication Data
Vickers, Rebecca
   Making better sentences. -- (Find your way with
   words)
   1. English language--Sentences--Juvenile
   literature.
   2. English language--Grammar--Juvenile
   literature.
   I. Title II. Series
   425-dc23

Acknowledgements
We would like to thank the following for
permission to reproduce photographs:
Alamy pp. 25 (© Jamie Carstairs), 29 (© David
Anthony), 51 top (© Everett Collection Inc); Art
Resources p. 7 (RKO / THE KOBAL COLLECTION);
Flickr p. 5 (© Crystal R. Williams); Getty Images
p. 41 (Digital Vision); Newscom pp. 17 (Album /
Documenta), 48 (AFP/Getty Images); Shutterstock
pp. 4 (© ARENA Creative), 8 (© Andresr), 10
(© margouillat photo), 13 (© alehnia), 15
(© CREATISTA), 19 (© Heike Rau), 20 (© Goodluz),
21 (© forbis), 23 (© Abramova Kseniya), 24 (©
Cathleen A Clapper), 27 (© Georgios Kollidas), 31
(© Action Sports Photography), 33 (© Maxisport),
35 (© Carlos Caetano), 37 (© YanLev), 40 (©
Stephane Bidouze), 42 (© Artisticco), 43 (© iofoto),
43 inset (ArTono), 44-45 (© Jan Martin Will), 51
bottom (© Alexey Stiop), Superstock pp. 11 (Stock
Montage), 14 (Cusp), 38 (Exactostock).

Back cover photograph of a golden retriever
reproduced with permission of Shutterstock (©
margouillat photo).

We would like to thank Joanna John for her
invaluable help in the preparation of this book.

Every effort has been made to contact copyright
holders of material reproduced in this book. Any
omissions will be rectified in subsequent printings
if notice is given to the publisher.

Disclaimer
All the internet addresses (URLs) given in this
book were valid at the time of going to press.
However, due to the dynamic nature of the
internet, some addresses may have changed, or
sites may have changed or ceased to exist since
publication. While the author and publisher regret
any inconvenience this may cause readers, no
responsibility for any such changes can be
accepted by either the author or the publisher.

Contents

Let's communicate

The way language is used is all about communication. In a school essay, you communicate how much you know and understand about a subject. A thank-you note communicates appreciation and love. A text message to a friend might communicate plans to meet or the latest gossip. All these forms of writing have their own styles and practices.

Following the rules

All languages have rules and conventions that you follow to make communication clear and easy to learn. In English, the rules of grammar help you say what you want in a way that your audience can understand. This is true whether the readers and listeners are teachers, employers, relatives, friends, or even strangers you will never meet who read your blog or chat with you online. The attention paid to the word order and structure of the sentences used, called syntax, can help or hinder you in the process of communication.

One of the newest forms of written communication is the weblog, usually shortened to blog. "Blogs" are like diaries or journals available on the internet and have been around since 1997. They can be general or relate to a particular interest of the writer, such as politics, fashion, science fiction, travel, music, or even blogging itself!

Graffiti walls in schools, colleges, and youth clubs promote instant communication. Legal spaces like this allow writers to have access to anyone willing to read their opinions on any subject. Some school and college graffiti walls allow departing students to "sign-off" with a comment before leaving.

Breaking the rules

The fact that there are rules about how sentences should be formed and words used doesn't mean you have to be boring. You just need to remember whom you are communicating with and the purpose of the communication. The type of language used to thank a great aunt for birthday money will be very different from that used to text a friend. To be a successful communicator, you need to master contrasting styles for varied circumstances. For example, being creative can mean bending the standard rules of grammar.

Every kind of writing presents its own challenges.

QUICK TIP

Glossary

This book has a Glossary on pages 53–54. If you see a word you don't understand, check the Glossary to see if the word is there. If it isn't, try a good dictionary (see page 52 for advice on understanding dictionary entries).

The building blocks of writing

Words are the smallest bits of language that can be used with meaning. If you say Go! or Listen!, you are communicating with just one word. This style, similar to the way a baby first uses language, is not enough for most types of communication. Much more complex ideas and instructions can be conveyed by putting words together according to a recognized and accepted style. These strings of words are called sentences.

Subject and predicate

In order to be a complete sentence, a group of words used together must contain a subject and a predicate:

- Subject – This is the name given to the part of a sentence that contains the main noun and the words related to it. The subject "governs" (does) the verb action in the sentence: **The dog** [subject] **barks** [verb]. This word or group of words usually, but not always, comes at the start of the sentence. Here are some sentences showing the subject in bold:

  Hogwarts School features in all the Harry Potter books.
  Films starring Jim Carrey are usually comedies.
  Last month **a tornado** destroyed half the town.

- Predicate – This is the name given to the main verb and the words related to it. The predicate usually follows the subject in a sentence. When the sentence is a question, the predicate can be first or even split. In the following examples, the bold words are the predicate:

  Nathan **put the bike in the garage.**
  The band **often performs in outdoor arenas.**
  Who were the girls **skating with?**

The types of words in the subject and the predicate are known as parts of speech. Each of the parts of speech has a special function in a sentence and in the way it can combine with other words. This syntax is the way grammar rules control sentence structure.

What else does a sentence need?

A sentence also needs to start with a capital letter and end with a punctuation mark – a full stop, a question mark, or an exclamation mark. It might also need other internal punctuation. All of the words it contains should be correctly spelled, including any necessary capital letters. For it to be a good sentence, the words used should be the best choice for the intended meaning and be in the right order.

Very simple communication can get information across to a reader or listener. For more complicated concepts, more words, used in a structured way, are needed.

Me Tarzan, you Jane.

QUICK TIP

When is a sentence not a sentence?

Fragments are groups of words that do not form a complete sentence. They are often used in speech and very informal writing. For example, if you ask someone a question when speaking, the person's answer might be a fragment: Do you want to come with us to the theme park? Not really. Even though this is common and acceptable in conversation or in dialogue, it is NEVER acceptable in formal writing.

Four types of sentences

All sentences have to express a complete idea using a subject and predicate. Sentences can be divided into four types, defined by how they are used and the mood they express:

1. Declarative – This is a sentence that says something. It may state a fact or answer a question: Ramez wants to take driving lessons as soon as he is old enough.

2. Interrogative – This sentence type asks a question. Questions are asked by changing the word order and adding a question mark when writing. This change in word order is called inversion. Some interrogative sentences can be answered with a yes or no: Are you going snowboarding with Emma? Others require a specific answer. Sentences in the second category usually start with What, Where, When, How, Which, Who or Why. For example, Which bus will you catch?

3. Imperative – This kind of sentence tells the reader or listener to do something. It is an order or a command. Imperative sentences can start with a verb (for example, **Eat** your vegetables!) or be in the standard word order starting with a subject (for example, You **must** eat your vegetables). If the message is very powerful or urgent, then an imperative sentence should have an exclamation mark at the end.

4. Exclamatory – This sentence type expresses a mood of strong emotion, feelings, or surprise. The end punctuation in an exclamatory sentence is an exclamation mark: This is a fantastic beach for surfing!

The same information can be presented in all of the four different sentence types:

Declarative: The girl is playing the guitar.

Interrogative: Is the girl playing the guitar?

Imperative: You must play that guitar!

Exclamatory: Wow, you can really play that guitar!

Word type	Simple definition	Some examples
Noun	Word that names a person, place, thing, feeling, quality, or idea	woman, mountain, road, anger, height, freedom
Pronoun	Word that is used in place of a noun	you, me, her, who, these, everyone, himself
Adjective	Word used to describe a noun or pronoun	small, blue, eight, thrilling, smoky
Verb	Word that says what a noun or a pronoun does or what it is	go, drink, is, seem, demonstrate
Adverb	Word that describes or modifies a verb or another adverb	inside, slowly, later, too slow, impossibly
Preposition	Word that shows the relationship between a noun or pronoun and other words in a sentence	above, from, with
Determiner	Word that limits or modifies a noun	the, some, both
Conjunction	Word that joins other words, phrases, or sentences	and, but, or
Interjection	Word used, usually on its own with an exclamation mark, to express an emotion or surprise	Ouch! Help! Bang!

To find out more about the parts of speech and how to use them, see *Types of Words*, another book in this series.

Simple, complex, and compound sentences

The very simplest sentences are very short without much detail. The sentence The dog barked tells you about that event, but you don't know what kind of dog it is, whom it belongs to, when it barked, or if the barking disturbed anyone. For that information to be presented, the sentence needs to be more complex.

First, a main clause

A simple sentence is made up of just one subject and predicate. This is called a main clause. The whole sentence Cassie drank the mint tea is a main clause. This simple, main clause sentence can be made more complex by adding another clause. If the additional clause cannot stand on its own as a main clause sentence, then it is known as a subordinate clause. Sentences with both a main clause and a subordinate clause are called complex sentences. Here is the sentence from above, but now with a subordinate clause, shown in bold: Cassie drank the mint tea **until the cup was empty**. The clause until the cup was empty is subordinate as it is a fragment, not a complete sentence. Clauses, both main and subordinate, must contain a verb. If a group of words does not contain a verb, it is called a phrase.

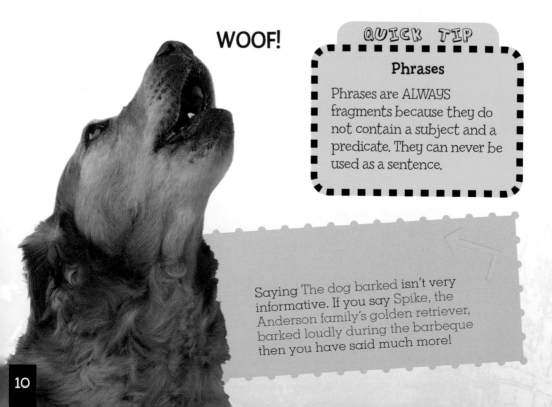

WOOF!

QUICK TIP

Phrases

Phrases are ALWAYS fragments because they do not contain a subject and a predicate. They can never be used as a sentence.

Saying The dog barked isn't very informative. If you say Spike, the Anderson family's golden retriever, barked loudly during the barbeque then you have said much more!

Type of phrase	Some examples
Noun phrase A noun phrase may be just one word, a noun, or many words. In the examples on the right, each added word is still part of the noun phrase which forms the subject:	**Your sister's boyfriend** was late for the party. **Your older sister's boyfriend** was late for the party. **Your older sister Nicola's boyfriend** was late for the party.
Adjectival phrase This can be an adjective on its own, or a group of words acting as an adjective. An adjectival phrase is used in a sentence to change or describe a noun:	**Green and white stripes** hung at every window.
Verb phrase This is the verb and the words related to it. The whole group acts as a verb. Here is an example:	Rosie **wants to buy a new smartphone.** It is possible for an additional verb phrase to not be the main verb of a sentence: **Having made her choice** [verb phrase], Rosie **took** [main verb] **the mobile phone to the shop assistant.**
Adverbial phrase Like an adverb, this changes or describes the verb:	Annika ran up the stairs **as lightly as a cat**. It tells the reader how Annika ran.
Prepositional phrase This starts with a preposition, such as around, beyond, in, or under. Here are a few examples:	The actors had to wait **under the bridge**. Every camera in the scene was pointed due west, **beyond the burnt-out car**. The director's assistant guided the male star **around the set.**

See if you can identify the types of phrases in this sentence. The answers are on page 55.

I then took off my spectacles, and, waiting about an hour till the tide was a little fallen, I waded through the middle with my cargo, and arrived safe at the royal port of Lilliput.

From *Gulliver's Travels* by Jonathan Swift (1667–1745), first published in 1726.

Subordinate clauses are dependent

Subordinate clauses depend on a main clause to be complete. There are four principal forms of subordinate clause:

- Relative, or adjectival, clause – This type of subordinate clause, attached to a noun or noun phrase, is either restrictive or non-restrictive. A restrictive clause helps identify what the noun refers to: The hotel **where we stayed** in Paris was very luxurious. A non-restrictive clause just gives some additional information about the noun or noun phrase: The hotel, **which has 110 rooms**, is centrally located.

- Complement clause – This type of clause is attached to a preceding noun, verb, or adjective. It is introduced by a word such as that or whether. Here is an example with the complement clause in bold: The view **that human actions cause global warming** is widely accepted.

- Adverbial clause – This type of subordinate clause behaves like an adverb and gives information related to place, time, cause, or condition: **As soon as the pool was empty**, the lifeguards locked the gate.

- Embedded and indirect question – This type of clause is a question which forms part of a larger sentence, but the full sentence doesn't have to be a question: Let me know **whom I should tell about the lost dog.**

WORDS IN ACTION

Building up meaning

Talented writers, such as American F. Scott Fitzgerald (1896–1940), use different clauses and phrases to build up their text, varying sentence length and sometimes using repetition for emphasis:

Let me tell you about the very rich. They are different from you and me. They possess and enjoy early, and it does something to them, makes them soft where we are hard, and cynical where we are trustful, in a way that, unless you were born rich, it is very difficult to understand. They think, deep in their hearts, that they are better than we are because we had to discover the compensations and refuges of life for ourselves. Even when they enter deep into our world or sink below us, they still think that they are better than we are. They are different.

From the short story "The Rich Boy" by F. Scott Fitzgerald, first published in 1926.

I hope my excellent use of subordinate clauses is really catching the crowd's attention.

The emperors, senators, and generals of ancient Rome were famous for their speeches. Their use of language was aimed at convincing or inspiring their listeners. Today's politicians and business leaders do the same thing.

Compound sentences: two into one

A main clause is a complete sentence, so when there are two main clauses, there are two sentences. Sometimes it might be better to make the two sentences into one. This is called a compound sentence. Why would this be a good idea? First, too many short, choppy, simple sentences can stop written work from having a nice flow. Second, the ideas or information in the two sentences might be very closely related and, by combining the sentences, you make that clear. Third, the type of relationship between the two sentences can be made more obvious by how the sentences are combined.

Conjunctions combine things

The part of speech used to join together two main clauses into a compound sentence is the conjunction (see page 9). When these small connecting words (such as and, or, but, yet, and so) are used this way, they are known as co-ordinating conjunctions. This is because they are joining together clauses of equal importance. The conjunction used can have a great effect on the meaning of the compound sentence. It needs to be selected carefully. For example, Sarah loves chocolate muffins **and** Lucy likes croissants just states information about what the two girls like to eat. If you change the conjunction, then the two main clauses are shown as comparing the food preferences: Sarah loves chocolate muffins, **but** Lucy likes croissants. It is important to choose the conjunction that makes the compound sentence mean what you intend.

The conjunction or is often used in compound sentences which are questions giving a choice between two things: Do you want to go and eat now or do you want to go straight to the film?

Conjunctions like but are often used to contrast two points of view.

You may think you have all the answers, but I know better!

WORDS IN ACTION

Variety equals interest

Complex and compound sentences, combined with short simple ones, give variety and interest to works of fiction:

When he woke, he had a shock. It was still daylight, and as he sat up he found himself looking straight out to sea! He looked anxiously at his compass. Perhaps it had broken? But the needle moved as it should. For a moment he thought he had lost his way in the dark and had wandered round in a circle till he was back again in the neighbourhood of the town.

From *I Am David* by Anne Holm (1922–98), first published by Methuen & Co. Ltd in 1965.

Being compound and complex

The most complicated sentences can contain two or more main clauses and at least one subordinate clause. A sentence of this type is called a compound-complex sentence. For example, here is a compound-complex sentence with two main clauses and one subordinate clause: After the tiger escaped [subordinate], the zoo closed [main], and the local police were informed [main]. Sometimes a long, complicated sentence can be the best way to express an idea or report a lot of information. However, just because something is correct or allowed by the rules of grammar, it is not necessarily the best way to communicate. Read long sentences out loud to see if they make sense or if they would be better broken down in to smaller bits.

Never run-on!

A run-on sentence is one with two main clauses which are pushed together without correct punctuation or a conjunction to join them:

WRONG: I have my visa now I can go to China.

RIGHT: I have my visa. Now I can go to China.

RIGHT: I have my visa so now I can go to China.

Too long?

In the 18th and 19th centuries, writers used much longer sentences than are commonly used now. Sentences frequently contained 25–40 words, compared to today's average of about 14. The British novelist Charles Dickens (1812–1870) was well known for the length of his sentences, with the longest clocking in at 249 words! Here is a shorter example:

Having borne this flattering testimony to the merits of our dwelling-place, and having incidentally shown this tendency to call me "sir", Joe, being invited to sit down to table, looked all round the room for a suitable spot on which to deposit his hat – as if it were only on some very few rare substances in nature that it could find a resting place – and ultimately stood it on an extreme corner of the chimney-piece, from which it ever afterwards fell off at intervals. [84 words]

From *Great Expectations* by Charles Dickens, first published in 1860–1861.

American author William Faulkner (1897–1962) wrote long and complicated sentences in many of his books. Faulkner is currently recognized by the *Guinness Book of Records* as having the longest grammatical sentence in a published work of fiction. It is in his novel *Absalom, Absalom* and is 1,288 words long!

QUICK TIP

Semicolon to the rescue

The punctuation mark known as the semicolon (;) can be used to combine two main clauses into one sentence. See page 20 of this book or *Punctuation and Spelling*, another book in this series, for more information.

Deciding how to put words, clauses, and phrases together into sentences can be very simple or very complicated. Punctuation can help sort out the confusion.

Separating sentences

All sentences need end punctuation marks to finish them. In English, there are three: the full stop, the question mark, and the exclamation mark. Interrogatory sentences always need a question mark, exclamatory sentences usually end in an exclamation mark, and other sentences end in a full stop.

Using commas to separate the groups of words

The different clauses and phrases in a sentence – particularly when they represent different ideas or modify different parts of speech – are separated from each other using a comma (,). Here are various situations when you should use a comma for these purposes:

- Series or list commas – These are used to separate three or more individual words or groups of words in a type of list: Will bought tomatoes, lettuce, and cucumbers. Carmel goes to judo on Mondays, modern dance on Tuesdays, and swimming club on Thursdays. The groups of words can even be complete sentences, but there must be at least three, with the last element connected with a conjunction, such as and or or: Sarah chose the red curtains, Amy chose the striped curtains, and Emma chose the flowered blinds. Series or list commas are also used to separate descriptive words that modify a noun: The small boy's huge, orange, diamond-shaped kite flew highest. The use of the comma before the connecting word in a series list is sometimes omitted. Find out which style your school prefers and use that style in your writing.

- Commas with conjunctions to join two sentences – This type of comma can only be used with a joining or linking word, such as the conjunctions and, but, or, while, and yet. Here is an example: Rafael likes Chinese food, but he would rather have pizza. Both sentences are complete and could stand on their own. Remember, you can never have a comma between two sentences unless there is a linking conjunction.

    WRONG: I don't have time now, I'll go tomorrow.

    RIGHT: I don't have time now, so I'll go tomorrow.

- Bracketing or parenthetical commas – These commas mostly work in pairs to separate off a bit of information. This information is additional to the main idea of the sentence and can be taken out, leaving a complete sentence behind. In this example, the words inside the bracketing commas add extra information that interrupts the flow of the sentence: Our first hamster, a male named Chewy, lived for three years. Sometimes the extra words are in a phrase that appears at the beginning or the end of the sentence. In those cases only one comma needs to be used. At the beginning: Instead of an encore, the band came back on the stage and talked to all the fans. At the end: The best beach is at Gull Point, eight miles west.

The flavours of these cakes are chocolate, lemon, coffee, raspberry, and lime. Commas are used to separate out the items in a list like this one. The sentence would look very confusing without them.

The semicolon: two into one

Another punctuation mark used to separate words in a sentence is the semicolon (;). It is properly used in only two ways:

1. A semicolon can be used to separate two complete sentences that are both main clauses. It is never used between a main clause and a subordinate clause, when the punctuation mark used should be a comma. Only use a semicolon if the information in the two sentences is very closely related and therefore needs to be grouped together rather than being presented as two sentences: The vet examined the cat's paws for glass fragments; he also checked its tail.

2. On the rare occasion when a sentence already has many commas in it, then a semicolon can be used to mark an important break, or to separate out complicated lists. Here is an example: For their wilderness camping trip, the group need to take things to eat, such as eggs, bread, and fruit; things to keep warm, such as tents, sleeping bags, and groundsheets; and equipment, such as an axe, a folding spade, and matches. Remember, if a sentence is too long or confusing, it might be better to break it up and rewrite it.

Most digital grammar-check programs recognize punctuation and grammatical errors. There are also grammar apps, which include punctuation, available for tablets and smartphones. Remember, when making corrections based on one of these programs, examine the choices provided very carefully. There is no point in replacing one wrong usage with another that is also wrong.

Colon: adding and explaining

A colon (:) is a punctuation mark used in a sentence to show that the information following it helps to explain or add to the information. In most cases, there is a complete sentence before the colon, while the words after the colon can be another sentence, a list, or even one word: Chloe really loves jewellery: rings, necklaces, and particularly bracelets. The information before the colon is usually general, and the information after the colon gives more details, examples, or explanation.

Here is another example of how to use a colon. Geoff got all his climbing gear ready to go: ropes, karabiners, pickaxe, and his helmet.

The dash

A dash (–) is a punctuation mark used to separate off a part of a sentence that strongly interrupts the rest of the flow. In this way, dashes used in pairs are like bracketing commas, but the words they set off need to represent a more powerful break. However, like bracketing commas, it must be possible to "read around" the material inside the dashes. The rest of the words must form a complete sentence: When the two teams met, they both seemed sure of victory – there was no doubting it – because each of them was a group champion.

Sometimes the interruption doesn't come in the middle of the sentence, but at the end. When this is the case, only one dash is needed: Woody swore that the cake was already gone when he got home – at least, that's what he said. This use of a strong interruption of the text at the end of a sentence is a more informal style and is probably only appropriate in creative writing or dialogue.

Dashes and number ranges

The appropriate punctuation to use when representing a range of numbers or dates in certain circumstances is a dash, not a hyphen. For example, Mark Twain lived 1835–1910 is correct. In this case the dash represents the words from and to. So, it could also be written Mark Twain lived from 1835 to 1910. It is wrong to mix the two styles, so if the word from is used, then there cannot be a dash between the two dates.

WRONG: Mark Twain lived from 1835–1910.

QUICK TIP

Don't dash to use a dash

ALWAYS think carefully before using dashes. They are often not the most accurate or appropriate choice.

Round brackets

Round brackets (( )), which are also called parentheses, are punctuation marks always used in pairs. Like bracketing commas and dashes, they are used to separate bits of information from the rest of a complete sentence. Round brackets can be used to set off both strong and weak interruptions to the flow of a sentence: Sarah lived in a high-rise flat (with two balconies) just north of the centre of town. They can also be used to set off information that adds to a sentence, but cannot easily be written into it, such as dates: Winston Churchill (1874–1965) was Prime Minister during most of World War II (1939–45).

Hyphens or dashes?

Find out about how hyphens are used differently from dashes in *Punctuation and Spelling*, another book in this series.

Next are fences 11-13 – if we don't fall at this fence – then it's the gold medal – and time to celebrate.

The dash does have a use as a punctuation mark, but it needs to be used correctly and not too often!

That's too much dashing around.

Square brackets

Square brackets ([ ]) are punctuation marks that are always used in pairs. Their main use is to separate off information which is being added to a direct quotation. The material in the square brackets is not part of the quotation. Here is an example from a quote by economist John Maynard Keynes:

> But, like Odysseus, the President [Woodrow Wilson] looked wiser when he was seated.

To list or not to list?

Sometimes a list of ideas or points being made in a piece of writing can be more effective when separated out from the main text. Word processing packages on computers make this easy through the use of bullet point and numbered point features. Never overuse lists in your writing, including features like bullet points, and never use them to avoid writing full and interesting sentences that link well together.

Useful lists

There are many occasions where lists are the most appropriate way to get information across, for example, the ingredients in a recipe, or the materials needed for a craft project.

SIMPLE FRESH SALSA
Here is a recipe that is all chopping and no cooking!

Ingredients:
- 4 medium-sized ripe tomatoes
- 6 spring onions
- a handful of leafy coriander
- 4–5 chopped green jalapeños from a jar (optional)
- 2 x 15 ml tablespoons of lime juice
- salt and ground black pepper

Method
1. Get a chopping board, paring knife, chef's knife, and bowl for mixing and serving. Rinse and dry all the vegetables.
2. Finely chop the tomatoes and put in the bowl.
3. Finely chop the spring onions (including some of the green stems) and stir into the tomatoes.
4. Finely chop the coriander leaves and stir into the tomato mixture.
5. Cut up and add the jalapeños (optional, can be quite hot).
6. Add the lime juice and a little salt and pepper to the mixture and stir well.
7. Cover and let the flavours blend for about an hour, and serve with corn chips.

Apostrophe: the most misused punctuation mark

Some punctuation is used with individual words. If it is wrongly applied, then the meaning and the accuracy of an entire sentence can be affected. The apostrophe (') is an example of a punctuation mark used with individual words. It is probably the most misused of all punctuation marks because it is employed in two completely different ways. It is used to make contractions (e.g. aren't, he'd), where an apostrophe is used to replace dropped letters. It is also added to words with the letter s to show possession (e.g. Andrew's tennis racquet). For more information on how to use apostrophes and other punctuation marks, see *Punctuation and Spelling*, another book in this series.

Misuse of the apostrophe is something that can make written work look silly and mean the wrong thing. This is embarrassing if the mistake is shown in a public place, like the apostrophe catastrophe on this awning. Here, the first apostrophe is used wrongly, but the second one is correct!

Getting to grips with punctuating speech

Speech is one type of writing where normal sentence styles are changed and special punctuation is used, including quotations, conversation, and dialogue.

Direct and indirect speech

The way speech is used in a sentence, including its punctuation, depends on whether it is direct or indirect speech. Direct speech is exactly what someone says. The fact that it is someone's words needs to be recognizable in the writing, and the way this is done in direct speech is through the use of quotation marks. Here is an example: "Painting is the most important thing in my life," explained the artist.

If information is being reported in the sentence, but there is no direct quotation from anyone, then it is indirect, or reported, speech and does not need quotation marks: The artist explained that to him painting was the most important thing in his life.

Sometimes it might be effective to use a small part of what someone has directly said in the form of a quotation, and this should always be in quotation marks: The artist explained that in his life, "Painting is the most important thing". These two types are very useful when writing up interviews with people, or when writing newspaper or magazine articles.

When you use other sources in your writing, you need to acknowledge that the information comes from somewhere else and is not your own work, or you could be guilty of plagiarism.

QUICK TIP

What is plagiarism?

Plagiarism is copying someone else's words or ideas and pretending that they are your own. There are two ways to avoid this terrible mistake. First, put quotation marks around any direct quotations from another source and say where the quotation is from, using an approved referencing method. Second, if it is a specific idea, and not a direct quotation, you can mention the person whose idea it is in your writing, by using a referencing method, such as a footnote. Remember, not all facts need to be treated this way. For example, something that is very well known, such as a date or event, will not need this treatment unless you are directly quoting the information.

Surely everyone knows when I was born?

The information that George Washington was the first president of the United States and that his birth and death dates are 1732–1799 appears in thousands of sources. Therefore, you would not be committing plagiarism if you did not give your source. However, if you directly quoted the same information from a biography of George Washington using the author's words without showing that information in quotes and giving credit to the author, you are plagiarizing the author's work.

Writing down conversations

If you need to recount conversations or write dialogue to form part of a story, it is good to learn the special way it is presented in written form. There are a few rules used for this type of writing:

- All spoken direct speech is always enclosed in quotation marks.
- When writing shows conversation going back and forth between two or more people, each person's bit of the conversation starts on a new line, usually indented.
- If the reported speech sentence of a person is interrupted by information about who the speaker is, the interruption is set off in commas.
- If the speaker information is before the reported speech, then there is a comma after it. If this speaker information follows the speech, then the speech ends in a comma and the full stop punctuation for the sentence comes after the speaker information.
- If the speech is a question or exclamation, the speech needs to end in a question mark or exclamation mark, but there will still be a full stop after the speaker information.

Confused? Here is a bit of conversation from Stephenie Meyer's novel *Twilight* to show how conversation is laid out:

> "Never mind, then," he said hastily in a voice like velvet. "I can see that it's impossible. Thank you so much for your help." And he turned on his heel without another look at me, and disappeared out the door.
>
> I went meekly to the desk, my face white for once instead of red, and handed her the signed slip.
>
> "How did your first day go, dear?" the receptionist asked maternally.
>
> "Fine," I lied, my voice weak. She didn't look convinced.

From *Twilight* by Stephenie Meyer, published by Atom, an imprint of Little, Brown and Company, in 2005

QUICK TIP

Double or Single?

There are single and double quotation marks. Different book publishers have their favourite style. This series of books uses double quotes. If you need to mark off a quote within a quote, or a group of words within dialogue, use the most popular style for the first quote marks and then the less popular style inside: "I love mountain climbing," said Evie. "It always makes me think, 'Wow, I'm lucky to be alive,' every time I get to the top."

The actors in this school production of *Bugsy Malone* have learned their lines from play scripts that contain the dialogue. The punctuation used by the playwright helps the actors work out when to say their lines.

Using words well

One unique way speech is written down is in the dialogue for plays. Each character's words are provided, usually along with some stage directions. The name of the character appears above or just in front of the lines he or she speaks. This extract is from the beginning of Act 3, Scene 1 of *A Midsummer Night's Dream* by William Shakespeare (1564–1616):

> SCENE 1 The wood; Titania lies asleep
> Enter Quince, Snug, Bottom, Flute, Snout, and Starveling
>
> **Bottom**
> Are we all met?
>
> **Quince**
> Pat, pat; and here's a marvellous convenient place for our rehearsal. This green plot shall be our stage, this hawthorn-brake our tiring-house; and we will do it in action as we will do it before the duke.
>
> **Bottom**
> Peter Quince!
>
> **Quince**
> What sayeth thou, bully Bottom?

Sometimes your sentences will go wrong. In the next few pages, you'll find out how to avoid some common mistakes.

What are verb tenses?

Tenses are the different forms of a verb that relate to the time when something happens. If something is happening now, you write or speak in the present tense. If it has already happened, you use the past tense. If it hasn't happened yet, but is going to, you use the future tense. Here is an example using the verb jump:

The horse and rider jump the fence. [present tense]

They jumped the same fence last week. [past tense]

They will jump the same fence next week. [future tense]

Verb tenses

Many of the grammatical mistakes that are made in sentences have to do with using the right verb tense. In very simple sentences, it is easy to work out the verb form you want to use. However, in compound and complex sentences, with more than one verb, it can be more difficult to make the right choice. Here are examples of some problems with verb tenses and how to avoid them:

- In a sentence where two or more actions happen at the same time, all the verbs that describe the action must be in the same tense.

  RIGHT: I cycled to the supermarket and bought ice cream.

  WRONG: I cycle to the supermarket and bought ice cream.

  The second sentence is wrong because the verb form cycle is in the present tense and the verb form bought is in the past tense. In the first sentence, they are both in the past tense.

- When there is one or more main verbs and an auxiliary, "helping verb", in a sentence, all the verbs must be the same tense if the action described happens at the same time.

  RIGHT: Melissa thought she could jump the gap.

  WRONG: Melissa thought she can jump the gap.

  The second sentence is wrong because the verb thought is in the past tense, but the auxiliary verb can is in the present tense.

- Some conditional sentences that start with the word if describe something that needs to happen in order for something else to then take place. These open conditional sentences use two tenses because the wish in the second part of the sentence hasn't yet happened. It is in the future. Here is an example:

RIGHT: If you go [present tense] on the train, I will come [future tense] with you.

WRONG: If you will go [future tense] on the train, I will come [future tense] with you.

QUICK TIP

Understanding verbs

For more information about verbs and verb tenses, see another book in this series, *Types of Words*.

If the yellow car overtakes the blue one, it will move into the lead.
In this open conditional sentence, the fulfilment of the condition in the first half of the sentence leads to the statement in the second half becoming a reality.

Agreement in sentences

One of the most common ways in which the rules of grammar are broken in sentence construction relates to the concept of agreement. Agreement is the matching of words in a sentence or phrase with others according to number (singular or plural), gender (male or female), person (first, second, or third), or verb tense. Getting agreement wrong in a sentence makes it grammatically incorrect.

Making the nouns and pronouns agree

In English, the only way in which nouns need to agree with another word relating to gender is nouns with pronouns. For example, if you are talking about a bride, you would need to use female pronouns, such as her and she: The bride wore **her** white high heels all day, even though **she** found them uncomfortable.

Nouns and pronouns also need to agree within a sentence in terms of number. If the subject of a sentence is singular, then all of the pronouns used after it in the sentence also need to be singular, or the sentence is incorrect:

RIGHT: A **teacher** needs to be sure that **his or her** class is paying attention.

WRONG: A **teacher** needs to be sure that **their** class is paying attention.

The second sentence is wrong because the main subject noun, teacher, is singular and their is plural. If the phrase his or her seems an awkward way around the problem, this can be overcome by making both the subject noun and the pronoun plural: **Teachers** need to be sure that **their** classes are paying attention.

EAT YOUR WORDS

Who is he?

Sometimes a sentence can be grammatically accurate, but also be confusing or hard to understand. This is certainly the case when pronouns are used without it being clear whom it is they refer to. Here is an example: Sam and Luke argued for hours over the puppies. He thought that he had the best names, but he always preferred his own choices. In the second sentence, it is impossible to work out which of the boys the different he and his pronouns are meant to represent. For the structure of a sentence to work, it must be obvious which previously mentioned subject or object is being replaced by the pronoun: Daisy played tennis with Kate for hours. She was tired, but Kate wanted to play for longer.

Plural pronouns have no gender

In English, all personal plural pronouns do not tell you the gender of the person being mentioned, and can represent groups that are male or female. Even if you are talking about the girls in a synchronized swimming team, you would still use the pronouns they and their, because plural pronouns do not change based on gender: The **girls** in the team were all sure **they** could hold **their** legs upright at the same time.

In English, all plural pronouns have no gender and can represent groups that are either male or female: The girls [female plural] in the synchronized swimming team practised every day after school. They [plural, no gender] knew it was the only way to perfect their [plural, no gender] techniques.

Making nouns and verbs agree

Luckily, since English verbs do not have gender, getting the agreement right between the subjects and verbs in a sentence only relates to person and number. A verb must always agree with the person being used. "Person" in grammar covers three categories of nouns and pronouns: the first person (the one speaking or writing), the second person (the one being written or spoken to), and the third person (the one being written or spoken about).

All three persons can be singular or plural, and this number also must agree with the verb form being used. Here are a few examples showing agreement of subject and verb based on person and number: **I am** a guitar player [first person, singular]. **It is** a guitar [third person, singular]. **They are** guitar players [third person, plural]. Any sentence where the noun and verb do not agree is grammatically incorrect.

Using auxiliary verbs correctly

The three primary auxiliary verbs are be, have, and do. Others are can, may, must, shall, will, and ought. Often an auxiliary is used to create a certain voice, mood, or opinion: I **must** go. James **can** read. In a sentence using an auxiliary verb, the number represented by the subject (singular or plural) must also match the number represented by the auxiliary verb.

RIGHT: The boys are building a rocket to launch in the park.

WRONG: The boys is building a rocket to launch in the park.

In the second example, the auxiliary verb form is singular, but the subject of the sentence, The boys, is plural. This is not grammatically correct.

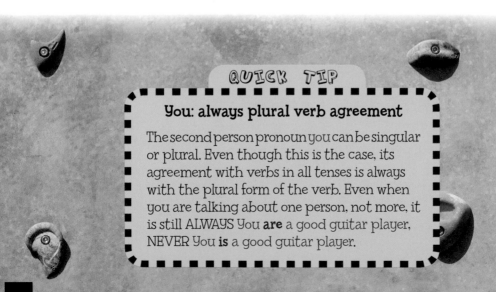

QUICK TIP

You: always plural verb agreement

The second person pronoun you can be singular or plural. Even though this is the case, its agreement with verbs in all tenses is always with the plural form of the verb. Even when you are talking about one person, not more, it is still ALWAYS You **are** a good guitar player, NEVER You **is** a good guitar player.

It is wrong to say They was climbing the wall, because the subject pronoun They is plural, and was is the singular form of the auxiliary verb. They do not agree. It is right to say They were climbing the wall. Both the pronoun and the auxiliary verb are in plural forms.

When to be active

A common criticism of the construction of a sentence is that it is "passive" or "in the passive voice". What does this mean, and when and how should it be avoided?

Be active, not passive

In a sentence written in the active voice, the subject of the sentence performs the action of the sentence. In other words, the subject directly carries out the action.

Here is an example: The courier delivered Abby's new tent. The subject, The courier, actively performed the action, delivered. It is very clear who is doing what. If the same sentence was written in the passive voice it would be this: Abby's new tent was delivered by the courier. In the passive voice the subject is now Abby's new tent. It doesn't perform any action. It passively receives the action, was delivered.

Active equals clear and direct

In English, the active voice is always the preferred style. It is clearer, more direct, and more forceful. Use of the passive can lead to awkward sentence construction, particularly in long, compound, and complex sentences.

PASSIVE: The tyre pressure was checked, and the bike mechanic also tightened the brake cables.

ACTIVE: The bike mechanic checked the tyre pressure and tightened the brake cables.

In the passive sentence, no direct information is given as to who checked the tyre pressure. That point is unclear. However, in the active sentence it is obvious that the bike mechanic performs both actions. The active voice always gives credit for the action to the performer of the action.

QUICK TIP

The verb To be

In its passive form, a verb needs to be accompanied by an auxiliary verb. For more information on auxiliary verbs, including the verb to be and all its different parts, see the book in this series, *Types of Words*.

You can recognize the active voice because it is the most like speech. We almost always speak in the active voice. For example, you would never say The bike was ridden to school today by me. You would say I rode my bike to school today.

Passive versus active

There are two occasions when it is acceptable to use the passive rather than the active form of a verb:

1. The sentence makes more sense without the person or persons who are doing the action being mentioned or repeated. For example, if you are writing about how a group of campers prepared an area for a weekend camp, it would be obvious and repetitive to keep saying The campers did this or The campers did that. Instead you could introduce a sentence in the passive voice, such as The site was cleared and the tents were put up.

2. You want to hide who performed an action or imply you do not know exactly how something happened. For example, It seems the milk carton was knocked over.

Getting your modifiers in the right place

In grammar, the term modifier is used to describe a word or group of words that has an effect on another word. A modifier can limit or add to another word's meaning. One way in which sentences can be awkward or unclear is if modifiers are used badly or positioned in the wrong place.

Single-word modifiers

There are three kinds of single-word modifiers: adjectives, participles, and adverbs. Most of these are straightforward to use and get in the right position.

- Adjectives are descriptive words that modify nouns or pronouns, and are usually placed in front of the words they modify. More than one adjective can be used to modify one noun or pronoun. Here is an example: The **comfortable, blue** sofa opened out into a bed.

More than one single word modifier can be used in a sentence: The **colourful, exciting flag** faces were **skilfully** painted.

- Participles are the -ing (as in boring) and -ed (as in dried) verb forms which can also can serve as adjectives. They are usually placed in front of the words they modify: The **talented** break dancer was drawing a crowd.
- Adverbs are words that modify verbs, adjectives, or other adverbs. They can answer a question, such as how, when, where, how often, or how much. Adverbs are usually placed directly after the verbs they modify. However, if the verb is followed by a direct object, then the adverb comes after the object: She followed the man **quietly**. When a sentence contains two or more verbs, the adverb needs to be positioned in the clause or phrase that contains the verb being modified. If this is not the case, then it can be confusing or even change the meaning of the sentence.

EAT YOUR WORDS

Position affects meaning

There are some words which can be adverbs or adjectives. They are placed depending on what word in a sentence they are modifying. The placement can have a strong effect on the meaning of the sentence - get the placement wrong and the meaning can be confused. You need to get it right for the sentence to mean what you want. These words include almost, always, just, never, and only. See below for example sentences with the different meanings:

Only Erin told me about the film party on Saturday night [used as adjective modifying Erin - meaning: no one else told me].

Erin **only** told me about the film party on Saturday night [used as adverb modifying told - meaning: she did not email or text in time, etc.].

Erin told **only** me about the party on Saturday night [used as adjective modifying me - meaning: I was the only one she told].

Erin told me **only** about the party on Saturday night [used as an adverb modifying the prepositional phrase about the party - meaning: that was the only thing she told me about].

Erin told me about the party **only** on Saturday night [used as an adverb modifying the prepositional phrase on Saturday night - meaning: that she didn't tell me any sooner than Saturday night].

Positioning phrase modifiers

As well as single-word modifiers, there are also phrase modifiers (see page 11) that need correct positioning in sentences. There are two main types of phrase that act this way:

- Prepositional phrases – These groups of words, which start with a preposition, can act as an adjective (modifying a noun or pronoun) or as an adverb (modifying a verb) in a sentence. When acting as an adjective, a prepositional phrase is usually positioned directly following the word or group of words it modifies: The singers **in the school jazz band** were all sixth-form students.

- Participial phrases – The -ed and -ing verb forms that act as adjectives can also function as phrases that start with participles. These phrases can be used as either adjectives or adverbs and can be placed in different positions in a sentence. Here is an example: **Yawning behind his hand**, Jared listened to the guest speaker. This type of phrase must be positioned correctly, or the sentence can be confusing and even comical: Jared listened to the guest speaker, **yawning behind his hand**. This makes it sound like even the speaker found his own talk boring!

Putting clause modifiers in place

There are two types of subordinate clause which function as modifiers for main clauses: the adjectival clause and the adverbial clause. Remember, all clauses contain a subject and a predicate.

If you write I want to see all the birds with binoculars, your reader will imagine the birds with binoculars watching you, not the other way around! It's much clearer if you rewrite the sentence as: I want to use binoculars to see all the birds.

Claire's friends would be happy to know that it is the dresses, and not them, that are many different sizes!

Adjectival clauses

These clauses, which modify nouns, start with that, where, which, who, whom, and whose. It is important for an adjectival clause to directly follow the noun or pronoun it modifies. If it is not positioned correctly, the sentence will be unclear and not make sense:

RIGHT: Claire bought multi-coloured dresses, **which were all different sizes**, as presents for her friends.

WRONG: Claire bought multi-coloured dresses as presents for her friends, **which were all different sizes**.

The misplacing of the adjectival clause in the second example has made the sentence ridiculous.

Adverbial clauses

These clauses, which modify verbs, all start with a subordinating conjunction, such as although, because, if, since, or when. It is easier to use these clauses, as they can be placed in various positions without causing the sentence to become unclear or mean something different:

Although he only sold a few, Brad continued to advertise his comic book collection online.

Brad, **although he only sold a few**, continued to advertise his comic book collection online.

Brad continued to advertise his comic book collection online, **although he only sold a few**.

Never dangle!

Dangling modifiers are a common error. They are created when a writer doesn't include all the information that should be in the sentence. The modifier is there, but where is the word or words that are supposed to be modified? Without them, the modifier is left dangling.

WRONG: Taking two aspirin, my headache disappeared.

RIGHT: After I took two aspirin, my headache disappeared.

WRONG: Driving towards the coast, the road was almost deserted.

RIGHT: Driving towards the coast, we noticed the road was almost deserted.

WRONG: Freezing after the snow storm, the house was warm and cosy.

RIGHT: Freezing after the snow storm, Leo found the house was warm and cosy.

The dangling modifier here makes it sound like this clever and speedy newspaper travels on its own! It should say: As I was running to catch the train, my newspaper fell onto the platform.

"Running to catch the train, my newspaper fell onto the platform."

QUICK TIP

Understanding the parts of speech

For more information about the parts of speech, such as prepositions, adjectives, adverbs, and conjunctions, see the book in this series, *Types of Words*.

Just look for the house with the river next to it made of bricks.

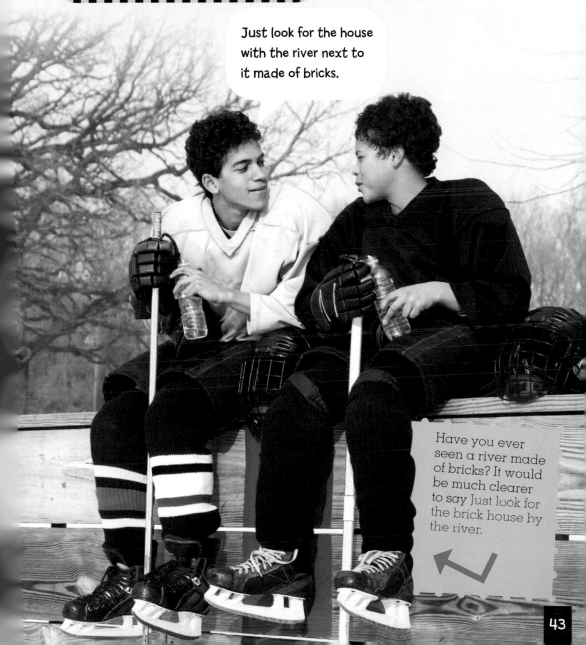

Have you ever seen a river made of bricks? It would be much clearer to say *Just look for the brick house by the river.*

Good sentences into good writing

Now that you know the basics of writing better sentences, and how to avoid the main pitfalls, here are more tips on how to become the best writer you can be.

When you are writing about a specific subject, such as global warming, you will need to think about specialist vocabulary to use, such as climate change, carbon footprint, and offsetting.

The right sentences for the purpose

When you are working out how to get an idea across in a sentence, there are four things you need to consider before you start:

1. Who is your audience? Are the sentences part of a school essay, a creative story, an article for the school magazine, an answer to an exam question, or an email to a friend you never see? You need to think about what kind of writing your reader is expecting.

2. What tone or style is your writing supposed to convey? Is it formal, informal, or even very informal? Formal writing for homework or school projects can be factual and informative, argumentative, or creative and imaginative. Maybe you have been given an assignment to write in a particular formal, literary style? Informal writing is usually more personal, and can show your opinions, emotions, and feelings. Very informal writing might use slang and not stick to grammar or spelling rules. Using the appropriate tone and style is crucial for successful writing.

3. What is the purpose of your writing? Is it meant to be informative research about a particular subject, or outline your ideas about a much debated issue? The purpose of the writing will also be affected by the audience and the tone. For school writing, you may be given very specific instructions about any writing you are expected to do, and you must think about the best way to follow these instructions before you write anything.

4. What kind of research knowledge and vocabulary will the sentences require? If you are writing about a specific subject, such as global warming, you may need to check out specialist vocabulary, as well as collect and use evidence, statistics, and quotations. If it is informal or creative writing, you may need to use direct or indirect speech.

Speaking versus written language

When people have informal conversations with each other, they often use all sorts of slang words, don't speak in perfect grammatical sentences, and put across their own individual style and personality. When you are writing for more formal purposes, your style has to be reflect this. However, if you are writing dialogue, or quoting exactly what someone has said, it is acceptable to reproduce how the speech would really sound. If you don't, then the speakers will not have their own personal voice. For example, many authors, such as Mark Twain, Harper Lee, and Charles Dickens, often wrote dialogue that reflected the accents, dialects, and level of education of their characters.

WORDS IN ACTION

Sounding right

In her famous novel *To Kill a Mockingbird*, American author Harper Lee (born 1926) reproduced various accents and modes of speaking found in the US southern states at the time the book was set. Each character has a recognizable personal voice:

> "I think I'll be a clown when I get grown," said Dill.
>
> Jem and I stopped in our tracks.
>
> "Yes sir, a clown," he said. "There ain't one thing in this world I can do about folks except laugh, so I'm gonna join the circus and laugh my head off."
>
> "You got it backwards, Dill," said Jem. "Clowns are sad, it's folk that laugh at them."

From *To Kill a Mockingbird* by Harper Lee, first published by William Heinemann Ltd. in 1960. Reprinted by permission of The Random House Group Limited.

QUICK TIP

Contractions

Many teachers think that contractions, such as can't, didn't, and isn't, should not be used in formal writing. Make sure to find out if this is the case in your school before you start any writing project.

There is nothing wrong with using very informal language in texts, tweets, some blogs, and emails. This is an area where you can express your personality and let your creative juices flow.

I kno I said id be able to cum with u 2moro, but who knew old ratbag Carson wld want those book reviews 1st thing Mon? Wknd now complete mess...hope u can forgive me. Wld ice cream at cafe on Mon help? I'll pay! :-) J xx

EAT YOUR WORDS
Formal vs. informal

When you are writing for school work, slang, informal language, over-personalization, and opinion may not be appropriate. No matter how much you might like your favourite author, it is never suitable to start a book review with something as personal, informal, and full of slang as Wow, Terry Pratchett, what a cool dude!

Using an outline

When you are pulling together the research you have done for a longer piece of writing, sometimes an outline can be a useful way to organize your work. An outline can be as simple as a list of numbered points in the order that information needs to be covered in your writing. It can be as complex as letters with subhead numbers, with further subheads working out the exact order and content of every paragraph. Turn the page to find out more ways to organize your ideas as you write.

Sentences into paragraphs

In most formal writing, there will be sentences that need organizing. For this purpose, you will need to turn logical groupings of sentences into paragraphs.

Supporting the topic

This paragraph is from a non-fiction work, a biography of the author Agatha Christie (1890–1976). It has a topic sentence (see page 49) followed by two sentences that support it:

> All her life Agatha was in love with her own childhood, and her family home Ashfield was the arena of her childhood dreams. She continued to dream about the house all of her life. When it was demolished in the 1960s, twenty years after it had been sold – perhaps proof that she had finally grown up – she cried like a child.

From *Agatha Christie: An English Mystery* by Laura Thompson, first published by Headline in 2007.

Popular authors often become the subject of biographies or books analysing their work. The English essays and book reviews you write for your schoolwork are part of this category.

Separating paragraphs

When you are writing by hand, paragraphs are usually separated from each other by indenting the first line of each paragraph. If the writing is being done on a word processor, then you can use the same indenting method or leave a skipped, blank line between each paragraph. Find out which style is preferred if you are writing for school.

Topic and then detail

Every paragraph in a longer piece of writing should be made up of a topic sentence supported by detail sentences. A well thought out paragraph with a central idea is the building block of all larger pieces of writing. In a factual essay or report, it is important to look back at the purpose of the piece of writing to make sure that every paragraph supports the aim. No topic sentence should be such a narrow idea that it is impossible to write anything about it. It also shouldn't be such a big idea that it needs far too many supporting sentences for one paragraph.

The order in which the paragraphs are placed should flow naturally, with no surprises. You cannot presume in an early paragraph that the reader knows something which is not going to be explained until three paragraphs later.

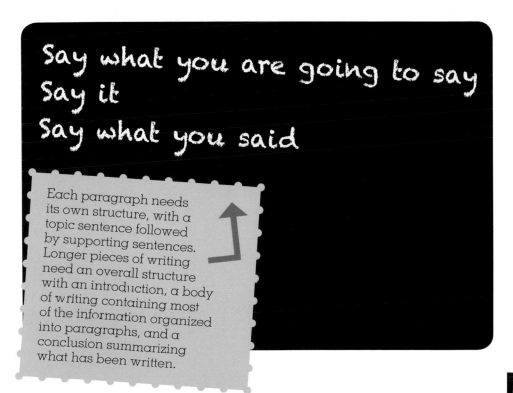

Say what you are going to say
Say it
Say what you said

Each paragraph needs its own structure, with a topic sentence followed by supporting sentences. Longer pieces of writing need an overall structure with an introduction, a body of writing containing most of the information organized into paragraphs, and a conclusion summarizing what has been written.

Variety and accuracy equals effective communication

To make your written sentences as good as they can be, they need to follow the rules of grammar and use well-chosen words in the right order. Words need to be spelled correctly and sentences should have the right punctuation and capitalization. They should have variety in their length and construction and, when necessary, be organized into meaningful paragraphs and longer pieces of writing.

Most importantly, sentences need to communicate what you want to say appropriately for the audience you have in mind. How good a sentence is depends on how well it fulfils its role of passing on your knowledge, your ideas, your thoughts, and your imagination.

Using a thesaurus

Sometimes in writing, it is hard not to repeat the same word in a sentence, or several times in a paragraph. If you have this problem and cannot think of a replacement word, try using a thesaurus. This is a book like a dictionary, but instead of definitions, for all the word entries it gives a number of synonyms: words that mean the same as the entry word. For example, if you are looking for a replacement for the word difficult, a thesaurus entry might list demanding, hard, and painful, among others.

There are thesauruses available online, in book form, or as tablet and smartphone apps. Remember, if you choose a word from a thesaurus that you are not familiar with, check its meaning in a dictionary in case it is not an accurate replacement for the word you want to change.

QUICK TIP

Avoid the cliché trap

The term cliché refers to any word, phrase, old saying, or idea that is overused to the point where it is trivial and meaningless. Using clichés can get a point across, but it is a lazy use of language. Some common clichés are live and let live, you can't teach an old dog new tricks, what goes around comes around, no smoke without fire, and 24/7.

Using words well

George Orwell (1903–1950), the famous British author of the novels *Animal Farm* and *1984*, was a creative writer who believed in the need for a formal structure of writing rules. He wrote many essays about the English language and writing. Here are three of his own rules he thought others should follow:

Never use a long word where a short one will do.

If it is possible to cut a word out, always cut it out.

Never use the passive where you can use the active.

From the article "Politics and the English Language" by George Orwell, published in *Horizon* in April 1946.

George Orwell followed many rules he thought would make his writing better. Can you think of one that would improve the way you write?

Using tired old clichés and overused words can make your writing seem boring. For example, one of the most overused adjectives at the moment is awesome. It is used to describe everything from a good burger to a theme park ride. Overuse has made its original meaning of "creating a feeling of awe" almost meaningless. Which word is now strong enough to describe the magnificent beauty of the American Grand Canyon?

Understanding dictionary entries

Dictionaries are reference books that list thousands of words and their meanings in alphabetical order. Good dictionaries can be found as books, websites, and as smartphone apps. There are also specialist dictionaries for individual subjects, such as medicine and art. Each full word entry gives the correct spelling of the word, any different spellings, the pronunciation, and the meanings or usages of the word. It might also include principal verb parts, plurals, and related words in the same word family. Sometimes information about the history of the word is provided. All of the abbreviations and pronunciation symbols used, and an explanation of how the entries are set out, is always given at the beginning of the dictionary. Here is a dictionary entry for the word photograph:

pronunciation and any alternate pronunciation divided into syllables with accent marks

parts of speech for the entry word

entry word

photograph (fō'tə gräf', -graf') *n.,v.,* **-graphed, -graphing**. *n.***1**. image taken by one of several photographic processes. *vt.* **2**. to take photograph of . *vi.* **3**. to practise photography. **4**. to be photographed or be the subject of a photograph. *The flowers photographed beautifully.* **photographer** *n.* **–photographic** *a.* **–photography** *n.* [*Gk* photo- +-graph 1839]

noun form word meaning

verb endings

transitive verb form word meaning

intransitive verb form word meanings

sentence showing usage of meaning

history of word, with language of origin of the parts and date of first use

other words in the same word family that also have entries in the dictionary

Glossary

accent stress placed on a syllable in a word

active voice verb form used when the subject of the verb is responsible for the action

adjective word used to describe, or modify, a noun or pronoun

adverb word that describes, or modifies, a verb or another adverb

agreement grammatical requirement that the form of a word or a phrase is determined by another word or phrase that it is linked with

apostrophe punctuation mark used as a sign of an omitted letter or letters, or to show possession

auxiliary verb, such as a form of be, have, or do, used with another verb. Auxiliaries are also known as helping verbs.

brackets pair of punctuation marks used to enclose words or figures

colon punctuation mark used before information introduced in the words that precede it

comma punctuation mark used in a sentence to create a short pause or separate off information

complex sentence sentence made up of both a main, independent clause and a dependent phrase

compound-complex sentence sentence containing two or more main clauses and at least one subordinate clause

compound sentence sentence which contains two or more main clause sentences connected by a conjunction

conjunction word, such as and, or, and but, that joins together words, phrases, or sentences

contraction shortened form of a word or shortened combination of two or more words

dash punctuation mark used to separate off a part of a sentence that strongly interrupts the flow

determiner word that limits or modifies a noun and is the first word in a noun phrase

dialogue conversation between two or more people or the spoken text of a script

exclamation mark punctuation mark used to show surprise or a strong emphasis

fragment part of a sentence that does not contain both a subject and predicate and cannot stand on its own

full stop punctuation mark used to indicate the end of a sentence

grammar rules that deal with the structure of the words and sentences in a language

grammatical relating to grammar

hyphen punctuation mark used to join words or parts of words

indent when the words in a line of writing are set in from the left margin

interjection word used to express an emotion or surprise, such as ouch! or help!

main clause part of a sentence containing a subject and predicate that can independently stand on its own

modifier word or group of words used to describe or limit the meaning of another word or group of words

modify use of a word or a group of words to describe or limit another word or group of words

mood grammar term that describes the attitude the speaker has about what is being said

noun word that names a person, place, thing, feeling, quality, or idea

number grammatical term which refers to the amount of something. The term singular means only one, while plural means more than one.

object word or group of words that receive the action of the main verb

parentheses see round brackets

participle the -ing and -ed verb forms

part of speech one of the types into which words are divided according to grammatical use

passive voice verb form used when the object receives the action of the verb

past verb tense used when describing a time earlier than the present

person term used to refer to the three categories of first person, second person, and third person

plural more than one

predicate part of a sentence made up of the main verb and words related to it

preposition word, such as above, from, and with, that shows the relationship between a noun or pronoun and other words in a sentence

pronoun one of the word types used in place of a noun

punctuation special marks used to mark sentences or words to make them clearer

question type of sentence that asks something which requires an answer

question mark punctuation mark used to show a sentence is asking something which requires an answer

quotation marks punctuation marks used to set off a direct quotation or spoken words, or to emphasize a word or phrase

round brackets curved pair of punctuation marks used to enclose words or figures

run-on term used to describe a sentence where two main clauses that could stand on their own are run together without proper punctuation

semicolon punctuation mark used primarily to divide two main clauses

sentence grammatical unit containing a subject and a predicate

singular no more than one

subject part of a sentence made up of the main noun and the words related to it

subordinate clause clause that cannot stand on its own as a main clause in a sentence

syntax structure of a sentence

tense way in which verbs mark time

thesaurus book that lists words that mean the same as other words

verb word that expresses the action or state of a noun or pronoun

Find out more

Books
Key Stage 3 English: The Scary Bits, Richard Parsons (CGP Books, 2009)

Key Stage 3 English: The Study Guide, Richard Parsons (CGP Books, 2009)

Organizing and Using Information (Information Literacy Skills). Donald Aldcock & Beth Pulver (Heinemann Library, 2009)

Oxford School Dictionary and Thesaurus (Oxford University Press, 2012)

Wordsmith's Guide to Paragraphs and Essays, Pamela Arlov (Pearson Education, 2008)

Write for Success (Life Skills), Jim Mack (Heinemann Library, 2009)

Websites
www.bbc.co.uk/schools/ks3bitesize/english/
This BBC website helps you revisit all the aspects of English you have studied at school.

www.bbc.co.uk/skillswise/topic/sentence-structure
Here you can explore in detail the structure of sentences, and how to make your own sentences better.

Help yourself!
There are many ways in which you can help yourself improve your skills in turning words and phrases into strong, meaningful sentences.
- Always read through anything you have written, even if it is just an email to a friend. You then have a chance to be sure you are saying what you intended.
- If you are worried about your written work making sense or being grammatically correct, try reading it aloud. If it doesn't sound right, it probably isn't.
- Keep a list of the things that your teachers flag up as errors in your writing. You can then use your list to check through any written work before you hand it in.

Answer to page 11:
I then **took off my spectacles** [verb phrase containing possessive noun phrase "my spectacles"], and, **waiting about an hour** [verb phrase containing prepositional phrase "about an hour"] till the tide was a little fallen, I **waded through the middle** [verb phrase containing prepositional phrase "through the middle"] **with my cargo** [prepositional phrase], and **arrived safe at the royal port** [verb phrase containing prepositional phrase "at the royal port"] of Lilliput.

Index